JULIA STILL_

Her Story, Unveiled: Motherhood, Struggles, and Hollywood's Complex Relationship with Icons

ROSEWOOD MEDIA

Copyright © 2023 by Rosewood Media

All rights reserved. Without the previous written permission of the publisher, no part of this publication may be copied, distributed, or transmitted in any form or by any means, including photocopying, recording, or other electronic or mechanical methods.

TABLE OF CONTENTS

INTRODUCTION — 5

CHAPTER ONE — 9

EARLY LIFE AND BACKGROUND — 9
EARLY PASSIONS AND INFLUENCES — 10

CHAPTER TWO — 13

THE BEGINNINGS OF AN ACTING CAREER — 13
"GHOSTWRITER" AND OTHER EARLY WORKS MARK A BREAKTHROUGH — 14
TRANSITION FROM CHILD TO TEEN ACTOR — 14

CHAPTER THREE — 17

RISE TO STARDOM: THE TEEN ICON — 17
THE INFLUENCE OF "WICKED" ON HER CAREER — 18
POPULARITY AND SUCCESS IN TEEN-FOCUSED FILMS — 18

CHAPTER FOUR — 21

MAINSTREAM AND CRITICAL ACCLAIM — 21
CHANGE TO MORE MATURE ROLES — 21
PARTICIPATION IN HOLLYWOOD BLOCKBUSTERS AND CRITICALLY ACCLAIMED PROJECTS — 22
PERFORMANCE EVALUATIONS IN "THE BOURNE SUPREMACY" AND "SILVER LININGS PLAYBOOK" — 23

CHAPTER FIVE — 25

ACADEMIC PURSUITS AND PERSONAL GROWTH — 25
ACADEMICS AND ACTING MUST BE BALANCED — 26
PERSONAL GROWTH DURING THIS STAGE — 26

CHAPTER SIX — 29

CAREER EVOLUTION AND RECENT PROJECTS — 29
IMPORTANT PROJECTS SUCH AS "RIVIERA" AND "HUSTLERS" — 30
OTHER DIVERSE ROLES & VOICE ACTING — 31

CHAPTER SEVEN — 33

CHALLENGES AND RESILIENCE — 33
OVERCOMING TYPECASTING AND INDUSTRY DIFFICULTIES — 34
CAREER RENEWAL AND ADAPTING TO CHANGE — 35

CHAPTER EIGHT — 37

PERSONAL LIFE AND OFF-SCREEN ACTIVITIES — 37
RELATIONSHIPS AND FAMILY LIFE — 37
PARTICIPATION IN CHARITABLE CAUSES AND ADVOCACY — 38
OUTSIDE OF ACTING, HOBBIES, INTERESTS, AND LIFE — 39

CHAPTER NINE — 41

LEGACY AND INFLUENCE — 41
AN EXAMINATION OF HER FILM AND TELEVISION CONTRIBUTIONS — 42
STILES' CULTURAL ICON STATUS — 43

CONCLUSION — 45

Rosewood Media

INTRODUCTION

Julia Stiles has been a key player in the cinema business for almost two decades, and her name is linked with range and depth in acting. Stiles has built a distinct place for herself in Hollywood, progressing from a teen idol in the late 1990s to a seasoned actor with a wide portfolio of parts. This introduction will offer an outline of her importance in the film business and hi

Highlight some of her most Notable Accomplishments

A. Teen Stardom and Early Promise

Julia Stiles started her acting career as a youngster, but it was during her adolescence that she became well-known. Her early performances in television shows like "Ghostwriter" revealed her innate acting talent and laid the groundwork for her future stardom. Her performances in movies like "10 Facts I Despise About You " and "Wicked" pushed her to teen idol stardom. These performances resonated with a generation of young viewers, making her one of the most recognizable faces in late-'90s adolescent movies.

B. Mature Roles Transition

Stiles effectively shifted from adolescent parts to more adult characters as she got older, demonstrating her ability to adapt and improve as an actor. Her performances in movies like "The Bourne Identity" trilogy and "Mona Lisa Smile" showcased her versatility and revealed that she was more than just a passing adolescent star capable of handling complicated parts. This time in her career not only cemented her reputation as a versatile actor but also broadened her appeal to a wider audience.

C. Awards and critical acclaim

Stiles' ability and dedication have not been ignored in the business. She has received several accolades and nominations, demonstrating her talent and devotion to her work. Notably, her performance in " The Playbook of Silver Linings " gained her critical praise and a Nomination for a Screen Players Union Award. This honor is a tribute to her ability to compete with some of Hollywood's most talented actresses.

D. Education and Personal Development Beyond Acting

Aside from her acting profession, Stiles has shown a strong devotion to personal development and education. She attended Columbia University and earned a bachelor's program in English literature, exhibiting her thirst for education and intellectual growth. Even at the height of her acting career, her pursuit of education says much about her character and goals.

E. Current Projects and Sustainability

Stiles has remained relevant in the business in recent years, taking on parts in television programs such as "Riviera" and engaging in projects that display her breadth as an actor. Her ability to adapt to new market trends while maintaining creative integrity is a characteristic of her ongoing popularity.

F. Philanthropic Activities and Advocacy

Julia Stiles is also well-known for her charitable activities and campaigning. Her engagement in projects such as Habitat for Humanity demonstrates her dedication to leveraging her platform to effect good change. This facet of her personality enriches her public presence and demonstrates that her influence goes beyond the silver screen.

G. Conclusion

Julia Stiles' career in movies is a story of progress, endurance, and variety. She has proven an enduring devotion to her profession, from dazzling audiences as a young star to pushing herself with complicated roles in her later career. Her success is judged not just by the parts she has performed or the prizes she has received, but also by her capacity to inspire and influence others both within and outside of the film business. Julia Stiles is a renowned and recognized person in Hollywood, whose career is a tribute to her skill and devotion, even as she continues to take on new projects and parts.

CHAPTER ONE

Early Life and Background

Julia Stiles, a famous actress noted for her mesmerizing performances and extraordinary flexibility, has a backstory that predates her meteoric rise to fame. Her upbringing and history are crucial in understanding the person and performer she became. This investigation digs into her upbringing, influences from her family, early hobbies, and the crucial years that created her.

Childhood and Family History

Julia O'Hara Stiles was born in New York City on March 28, 1981, to potter Judith Newcomb Stiles and businessman John O'Hara. Her parents owned and maintained a ceramics business in SoHo, Manhattan, where she grew up in a middle-class setting. Stiles' younger siblings are Jane and Johnny. This supportive and culturally diverse atmosphere was crucial in her early exposure to the arts.

Stiles was immersed in the rich and dynamic culture of New York City from an early age. Her mother's creative talents surely inspired her, instilling in her a passion for creation and expression. Her father's commercial expertise may have also instilled in her a sense of discipline and pragmatism, which helped to balance her creative interests.

Early Passions and Influences

Stiles' early interest in acting stems from a combination of innate aptitude and the culturally stimulating atmosphere of New York City. Her first excursion into the realm of performing occurred when she was 11 years old and started sending letters to Manhattan theater directors expressing her desire to act. This aggressive attitude reflected her early tenacity and enthusiasm for the profession.

Her early inspirations were the New York theater and cinema scenes, a city known for its cultural energy. A young Stiles' access to Broadway productions, street performances, and a varied assortment of cultural events gave a rich tapestry of inspiration. This experience had a significant impact on her creative sensibility and approach to acting.

Formative Years and Education

Stiles' education was a mix of conventional academics and creative experimentation. She went to the Professional Children's School in New York, which catered to young entertainers and athletes by enabling them to continue their professional vocations while still obtaining an education. This setting was critical in developing her burgeoning talent, as it provided a mix of academic rigor and creative flexibility.

Stiles was very engaged in theater throughout her high school years, both at school and in community shows. Her involvement in these early concerts was both a showcase of her skill and a valuable learning experience. It provided her with a practical grasp of acting, as well as the ability to experiment with various parts and improve her abilities in real-world situations.

Stiles also maintained an excellent academic record, displaying her commitment to education. Her academic studies were not overshadowed by her acting profession; rather, they complimented one another, enhancing her growth and development.

Stiles made a critical choice to continue her studies after graduating from high school, despite her burgeoning celebrity. She enrolled in Columbia University, demonstrating her dedication to academic progress. She managed her academic education with her acting profession while majoring in English Literature, demonstrating an outstanding ability to juggle both. Her time at Columbia was not just about academic performance; it was also about growing, exploring new ideas, and gaining a larger perspective on life and art.

Julia Stiles's early life and upbringing are a mosaic of family support, cultural exposure, early enthusiasm, and intellectual endeavors. Her upbringing in an artistically stimulating atmosphere, her proactive attitude to acting, her early theatrical experiences, and her dedication to study all contributed to her eventual success. These factors shaped her not just as an actress, but also as a well-rounded human with a profound love for art and a strong sense of self. These early experiences continued to affect her decisions, performances, and career in the film business when she entered the realm of professional acting.

CHAPTER TWO
The Beginnings of an Acting Career

Julia Stiles' acting career began with drive, skill, and a steady rise to stardom. Stiles' path in the acting field is defined by key milestones that affected her career trajectory, from her early parts to her breakthrough performances.

Early Roles and the Path to Acting

Julia Stiles' foray into acting was defined by a mix of natural skill and tenacity. At the early age of 11, she started her adventure into the world of acting by contacting theater directors personally in New York City, rather than via traditional means such as casting calls. This aggressive attitude landed her a role in the New York theatrical scene, where she earned valuable acting experience.

Her early responsibilities were little yet crucial. She performed in a few commercials and non-speaking roles in films, which gave her valuable experience working on a professional set. These early experiences were crucial in teaching her the intricacies of acting as well as the dynamics of the film and television industries.

"Ghostwriter" and Other Early Works Mark a Breakthrough

Julia Stiles got her big break in the children's television series "Ghostwriter," which ran on PBS from 1992 to 1995. She portrayed Erica Dansby in "Ghostwriter," a girl who was part of a gang of young detectives who solved mysteries with the assistance of an unseen ghost. This was an important part of her career since it was her first big on-screen performance and it exposed her acting abilities to a larger audience.

Following her appearance on "Ghostwriter," Stiles proceeded to take on parts that might further her acting career. She appeared in episodes of various television series and had minor parts in films. While not yet major roles, each of these roles contributed to her reputation as a young and budding actress in Hollywood.

Transition from Child to Teen Actor

The shift from child to adolescent parts is sometimes a difficult era in many performers' careers, but Julia Stiles handled it with elegance and intelligent decisions. As she approached her adolescence, she began to take on increasingly challenging and adult responsibilities.

One of her most notable teen performances was in the 1998 film "Wicked," in which she portrayed a disturbed adolescent. This portrayal was a change from her previous, more innocent parts, and it demonstrated her ability to tackle more nuanced and emotionally challenging roles. It was a crucial stage in her transformation from kid to adolescent fame.

The actual turning point in Stiles' career came with the 1999 teen romantic comedy film "10 Facts I Despise About You," in which Kat Stratford was played by her., a clever and independent adolescent in Shakespeare's "The Controlling of the Shrew." Her performance in the film was critically appreciated, and it is largely regarded as her breakthrough role. The picture not only thrust her into the spotlight but also established her as a major young actor.

Julia Stiles' acting career began with a mix of early chances, her aggressive attitude to obtaining jobs, and a sequence of performances that demonstrated her riding skills. From her debut part in "Ghostwriter" to her move into adolescent roles in films like "Wicked" and "10 Things I Hate About You," Stiles exhibited an extraordinary ability to adapt and improve as a performer. These formative years provided the groundwork for her successful Hollywood career and paved the way for the numerous parts she would play in the future.

Her rise from child performer to adolescent celebrity is a tribute to her skill, determination, and shrewd professional decisions.

CHAPTER THREE

Rise to Stardom: The Teen Icon

Julia Stiles' career shifted from a promising young actress to a teen idol in the late 1990s, a time defined by major performances that connected with a young audience and established her as a noteworthy figure in Hollywood.

Key Positions in the Late 1990s

Julia Stiles rose to fame in the late 1990s with a string of performances that displayed her ability and flexibility as an actor. Stiles started to take on more major roles in films that appealed to a youthful audience after her first success in television and modest film appearances. Her selections ranged from indie films to big Hollywood movies, enabling her to demonstrate her versatility as an actor.

Her first major film performance was in "The Devil's Own" (1997), in which she had a minor role. Despite not being a prominent part, it was noteworthy since it signified her crossover to a more popular film. Her later flicks, however, cemented her status as a teen idol.

The Influence of "Wicked" on Her Career

The 1998 film "Wicked" marked a watershed moment in Stiles' career. In this psychological thriller, she played a manipulative and tormented adolescent, a break from the more innocent roles she had previously played. Her performance in "Wicked" was praised by critics and displayed her ability to play complicated, dark characters. This role not only pushed her as an actor but also broadened her appeal to a broader audience, demonstrating that she could go beyond usual adolescent roles.

"Wicked" had a significant impact on her professional path. It allowed her to exhibit her acting abilities while also opening opportunities for more varied and demanding assignments. This film was crucial in breaking her out of the stereotype of an adolescent actor, paving the path for her future success.

Popularity and Success in Teen-Focused Films

Stiles rose to prominence in adolescent film in the late 1990s. Her performance in the 1999 film "10 Things I Hate About You" was a watershed moment in her career. Stiles portrayed Kat Stratford, a brilliant, assertive, and strong-willed adolescent in this contemporary rendition of Shakespeare's "The Controlling of the Shrew." The film was a financial and critical success, with Stiles' performance receiving special attention. Her depiction of Kat connected with the film's youthful audience and cemented her status as a teen idol.

"10 Things I Hate About You" was a cultural phenomenon of its day, not merely a successful adolescent film. The film's popularity aided Stiles' developing star, making her a household figure among young viewers. It also showed her ability to carry a film as the main actor, highlighting her charm and screen presence.

Following the popularity of "10 Facts I Despise About You," Stiles continued to play teen-oriented parts in films. She co-starred in the film "Down to You" (2000), and she co-starred alongside Freddie Prinze Jr. another hit film that established her image as a teen superstar. Her ability to represent individuals that were relevant to the youth of the day contributed significantly to her appeal.

Stiles' success in teen-oriented films reflected not just her acting ability but also her mastery of the genre. She avoided the problems of one-dimensional young characters by choosing parts that were diverse and multidimensional. Her performances were subtle and realistic, allowing her characters to stand out and be remembered.

Julia Stiles' career was transformed in the late 1990s when she rose to prominence as a teen superstar. Her significant performances at this time, particularly in films like "Wicked" and "10 Facts I Despise About You," were pivotal in developing her career. These films not only displayed her brilliance but also her ability to connect with a youthful audience. Her success in these teen-oriented films paved the way for her subsequent success in Hollywood, establishing her as a versatile and skilled actor. Her meteoric rise during this period is a credit to her talent, character selection, and awareness of the complexities of the adolescent cinema genre.

CHAPTER FOUR

Mainstream and Critical Acclaim

Julia Stiles' transformation from adolescent idol to renowned actor in mainstream and highly praised films was a huge step forward in her career. This phase is distinguished by her transition into more adult roles, involvement in blockbuster films, and highly lauded performances, most notably in " The Supremacy of Bourne " and "Silver Linings Playbook."

Change to More Mature Roles

Stiles moved away from the adolescent genre and into more varied and demanding parts in the early 2000s. This change was critical for her career since it displayed her versatility as an actor and her ability to appeal to a larger audience. She started to take on more challenging and adult parts, moving away from the adolescent dramas that had dominated her early career.

During this time, her project selection represented a conscious plan to diversify her portfolio. Stiles expressed a desire for jobs that pushed her as an actor, looking for opportunities to explore new character relationships and narrative intricacies.

Participation in Hollywood Blockbusters and Critically Acclaimed Projects

Stiles' involvement in the "Bourne" film series was one of the most important components of her career in the 2000s. Stiles portrayed Nicky Parsons, a CIA officer, beginning with "The Bourne Identity" (2002) and continuing with "The Bourne Supremacy" (2004) and "The Bourne Ultimatum" (2007). Her participation in this hit series was a significant stride into mainstream film, enabling her to reach a worldwide audience.

Stiles' ability to hold her own in a large Hollywood production was highlighted in "The Bourne Supremacy," a high-profile film. Her performance as Nicky Parsons was nuanced, adding dimension to a supporting character and adding to the film's overall complexity. Stiles' performance was acclaimed for its nuance and power, demonstrating that she could smoothly switch from adolescent dramas to action-packed blockbusters.

Stiles' part in the 2012 film "Silver Linings Playbook" was another watershed moment in her career. She portrayed Veronica, the sister of the female protagonist, Jennifer

Lawrence, in this highly praised film. Stiles' performance, while being in a supporting part, was noteworthy for its intricacy and emotional depth.

"Silver Linings Playbook" was a critical and financial success, winning multiple awards and honors. Stiles' participation in such a high-caliber film not only highlighted her acting abilities but also cemented her place as a versatile and renowned actress in Hollywood.

Performance Evaluations in "The Bourne Supremacy" and "Silver Linings Playbook"

Stiles' depiction of Nicky Parsons in "The Bourne Supremacy" was a major plot point. Her character's progression from a minor operative in the first film to a more significant position in the sequels was handled with subtlety and complexity. Nicky was a recognizable and appealing character in a genre dominated by masculine protagonists and action scenes, because of Stiles' portrayal of fragility and courage.

Stiles displayed her capacity to contribute considerably to a film even in a little part in "Silver Linings Playbook." Her performance as Veronica was defined by a combination of aggressiveness and compassion, serving as a counterbalance to the film's more colorful characters. Her performance gave depth to the film's depicted family relationships and demonstrated her flexibility as an actor.

Julia Stiles' transformation from adolescent idol to actress renowned for roles in popular and critically acclaimed films demonstrates her brilliance, adaptability, and shrewd career decisions. Her move to more adult parts enabled her to show off her acting versatility and appeal to a larger audience. Her performances in movies similar to "The Bourne Supremacy" and "Silver Linings Playbook" proved her versatility and ability to give nuanced portrayals in a variety of genres. This period of her career cemented her status as a renowned Hollywood figure and demonstrated her development and progress as an actor.

CHAPTER FIVE
Academic Pursuits and Personal Growth

While establishing herself as a successful Hollywood actress, Julia Stiles made a major choice that distinguished her from many of her peers: she opted to seek further education. This choice, as well as her academic career, provide insight into her character, goals, and personal progress throughout this period.

The Decision to Continue Your Education

Stiles' choice to attend college was a pleasant departure from a profession known for its superficiality. Following her early success in movies throughout her adolescence, she elected to attend Columbia University, an Ivy League institution. This choice to seek higher education was more than simply a desire to get a diploma; it was a statement about the importance she put on learning and personal growth.

Her major, English literature, promotes her academic interests even more. This topic of study, rich in analysis, critical thinking, and human nature inquiry corresponds well with her acting profession, where comprehending complicated characters and tales is vital.

Academics and Acting must be Balanced

Balancing a budding acting career with the requirements of an Ivy League degree was no easy task. Stiles handled this difficult dual responsibility with grace and dedication. Her ability to balance production schedules, promotional trips, and a demanding academic burden demonstrates her discipline and time management abilities.

This balancing task required not just practical modifications such as scheduling and prioritizing, but also a mental and emotional balance of two worlds. There was the flashy and fast-paced world of Hollywood on one side, and the academically rigorous and introspective atmosphere of university on the other.

Personal Growth During This Stage

Stiles' time at Columbia was not simply about academics; it was also about important personal development. As a student, she was able to examine ideas, ideologies, and books that enlarged her worldview. It gave her a break from the constant glare of Hollywood, giving her a sense of normality that is sometimes elusive in the entertainment world.

Furthermore, her experience in college is likely to have contributed to her depth as an actor. Engaging in different reading and critical thinking would have broadened her awareness of human psychology, emotions, and social topics, all of which are necessary skills for any actress.

Furthermore, Stiles was able to build an identity apart from her acting job during this time in her life. It allowed her to develop as a person, not only as a public personality. This distinction is critical in an industry where personal and public personalities sometimes merge and become indistinguishable.

Julia Stiles' willingness to seek further education and her ability to reconcile it with her acting profession demonstrate her commitment to personal development and intellectual improvement. Her tenure at Columbia University was a time of great personal and professional growth for her. It demonstrated her dedication to her principles, her discipline in juggling several tasks, and her drive to learn more about the world. This period in her life not only enriched her depth as an actor but also shaped her into a well-rounded and grounded person.

CHAPTER SIX
Career Evolution and Recent Projects

Julia Stiles' career trajectory in the late 2000s and early 2010s was marked by a considerable move away from mainstream filmmaking and into more diversified parts in television and indie films. This change displays her flexibility as an actor and her eagerness to explore other aspects of the performing business.

A Shift Away from Mainstream Cinema and Toward Television and Indie Films

Stiles decided to broaden her career after her success in blockbuster blockbusters and teen-focused films by taking on parts in television and indie films. This transition allowed her to experiment with other sorts of characters and narrative approaches. Independent films can provide more complicated, nuanced roles and creative flexibility than mainstream filmmaking, which aligns nicely with Stiles' artistic views.

Stiles discovered a platform in television to dig into character-driven storylines that build over a longer period, as opposed to the relatively succinct narrative approach of cinema. This medium allowed her to go deeper into her roles and demonstrate her versatility as a performer.

Important Projects such as "Riviera" and "Hustlers"

Stiles' major television projects include the British series "Riviera" (2017-2020), in which she portrayed Georgina Clios, a woman navigating the hazardous and glamorous world of the French Riviera. Her performance in "Riviera" received much praise, demonstrating her ability to carry a series as the protagonist. The success of the program solidified her reputation as a varied and brilliant actor.

Another notable accomplishment in Stiles' recent career is the 2019 crime thriller "Hustlers," in which she plays a journalist who investigates a gang of former strip club workers. Stiles' portrayal in "Hustlers" was praised for its sincerity and depth. The film's success was a watershed moment in her career, showcasing her capacity to flourish in a variety of cinematic genres.

Other Diverse Roles & Voice Acting

Stiles has moved into voice acting, demonstrating her flexibility and desire to explore many elements of her trade. Voice acting demands a distinct set of talents from on-screen acting since it relies heavily on voice expression to communicate emotions and stories.

Stiles continues to take on a range of parts in various indie films and television projects, each exhibiting a distinct facet of her acting ability. These parts helped her to continue developing as an actor, as she was continuously challenged with new and different characters.

Julia Stiles' career trajectory and recent ventures demonstrate her versatility and dedication to her profession. Her move from mainstream filmmaking to television and indie films illustrates her eagerness to experiment with different roles and narrative mediums. Projects like "Riviera" and "Hustlers," as well as her move into voice acting, demonstrate her versatility as an actor and her capacity to reinvent herself. This stage of her career demonstrates her adaptability, perseverance, and persistent love of performing.

Rosewood Media

CHAPTER SEVEN
Challenges and Resilience

Julia Stiles' path in the film business is a riveting story of perseverance and adaptability in the face of adversity. Her career, which has been distinguished by both highs and lows, gives insight into the complexity of Hollywood and the tenacity necessary to effectively traverse it.

Discussing Her Career's Ups and Downs

Stiles' career took off quickly, with her seamless shift from child performer to adolescent celebrity in the late 1990s. Stiles, like many other performers who acquired early popularity, had the problem of developing her profession as she grew older. She continued to prosper in the early 2000s, with parts in high-profile movies similar to the "Bourne" series. Despite her accomplishments, Stiles also had moments where her career seemed to stall, which is a regular occurrence given the cyclical nature of Hollywood.

This dip in her career may be linked to several causes, including the inherent difficulties of transferring from juvenile roles to adult ones, as well as the ever-changing preferences of moviegoers. During these calmer moments,

Stiles made a deliberate choice to pursue options outside of the mainstream Hollywood spotlight, such as furthering her schooling and auditioning for parts in indie films and theater.

Overcoming Typecasting and Industry Difficulties

The prospect of being typecast was one of the most critical issues Stiles faced. She had to work hard to exhibit her breadth as an actor since she was mostly known for her parts in adolescent dramas and rom-coms. Stiles dealt with this by taking on parts that were diverse and demanding, moving away from the adolescent type that had dominated her early career.

Her roles in films such as "The Business of Strangers" and "Mona Lisa Smile," as well as her involvement in the "Bourne" series, demonstrated her ability to play more complicated and sophisticated characters. These parts served to debunk the misconception that she was only appropriate for particular types of roles, demonstrating her range and depth as an actor.

Stiles also had to deal with the traditional obstacles of the Hollywood business, such as severe rivalry for parts, the pressure to adhere to specific standards, and the necessity to continuously reinvent oneself to be relevant. Her continuing success in the profession is credited to her skill, perseverance, and adaptability to market expectations.

Career Renewal and Adapting to Change

Stiles' career has recently taken a turn for the better, with appearances on television and in indie films. Her main roles in "Riviera" and "Hustlers" are good instances of her revival. These endeavors enabled her to showcase her persistent brilliance and popularity, as well as her versatility in many forms and genres.

Stiles' ability to negotiate Hollywood's shifting environment, with the emergence of streaming services and the increased significance of television as a platform for high-quality programming, demonstrates her versatility and industry knowledge. She has effectively moved from a teen idol to a renowned actress in both cinema and television, an accomplishment that requires not just skill but also a thorough knowledge of the industry's dynamics.

Julia Stiles' career, with its ups and downs, struggles, and eventual resurgence, demonstrates her perseverance and flexibility. Her experience highlights the challenges of working in a competitive and rapidly changing sector. Stiles has remained relevant and successful in Hollywood by constantly adapting, accepting new challenges, and displaying her flexibility as an actor. Her professional history exemplifies how skill, along with dedication and adaptation, can lead to long-term success in the film business.

CHAPTER EIGHT
Personal Life and Off-Screen Activities

Julia Stiles has a complex and diverse personal life further to her excellent professional career. Her family life and relationships, her engagement in different philanthropic causes and campaigning, and her interests and hobbies outside of performing are all part of her journey.

Relationships and Family Life

Julia Stiles has always kept her personal life private, a posture that reflects her desire to keep her off-screen life apart from her public image. This choice for solitude has allowed her to preserve a level of normality that is sometimes lacking in superstars.

When she met camera assistant Preston J. Cook on the set of "Blackway" in 2015, her family life took a big change. The pair got engaged in 2016 and married in a private ceremony in 2017. Strummer Newcomb Cook, Stiles and Cook's first child, was born in October 2017. Her child's birth signaled the beginning of a new chapter in her life, as she embraced parenthood with the same fervor and dedication she had shown in her professional achievements.

Being a mother has surely given Stiles' life a new dimension, changing her priorities and daily routine. Balancing parenthood and her job has been a struggle for Stiles, who has managed to maintain a successful career while being a hands-on mom.

Participation in Charitable Causes and Advocacy

Apart from her acting profession and family life, Stiles has been engaged in several humanitarian initiatives and advocacy activities. Her dedication to social concerns shows her desire to utilize her platform for good change and to make a significant contribution to society.

Habitat for Humanity, an organization that helps create affordable homes for individuals in need, is one of her favorite causes. Stiles has been an active participant in their efforts, including physically engaging in house building. This hands-on approach to charitable work reflects her determination to make a real impact in the lives of others.

Stiles has shown an interest in education-related topics and other social concerns further to her work with Habitat for Humanity. Her advocacy activity demonstrates her conviction in leveraging her power to assist vital causes and raise awareness about challenges affecting communities worldwide.

Outside of acting, Hobbies, Interests, and Life

Stiles' personal life is as varied and intriguing as her professional life. In her spare time, she pursues a diverse variety of interests and activities, which contribute to her well-rounded personality.

Writing is one of her well-known passions. Stiles has acknowledged an interest in writing, which corresponds to her academic background in English literature. Writing gives her a creative outlet other than performing, enabling her to express herself in new ways.

Stiles also enjoys traveling and learning about various cultures. Her travel experiences broadened her perspective and gave her a better grasp of the world. This passion for travel and adventure acts as a source of relaxation and pleasure for her, as well as inspiration for her artistic endeavors.

Julia Stiles' personal life and off-screen activities reveal a well-rounded person who values privacy, family, and civic duty. Her dedication to her family, active engagement in philanthropic organizations, and numerous interests outside of performing all add to her public presence. These elements of her life create a more complete picture of who she is outside of the spotlight, revealing her as a multifaceted character with a strong dedication to her ideals and societal well-being.

CHAPTER NINE
Legacy and Influence

Julia Stiles' impact and influence in the film business stretch well beyond her on-screen performances. Her influence on the business and emerging actors, as well as her considerable achievements in cinema and television, have sealed her position in Hollywood history.

The Influence on the Film Industry and Young Actresses

Julia Stiles broke into the film business at a period when adolescent dramas and romcoms were very popular. Her choice of parts in the late 1990s and early 2000s, which featured strong, autonomous female characters, established a new norm for young Hollywood actors. Stiles' depiction of multidimensional and varied characters in films such as "10 Things I Hate About You" and "Save the Last Dance" was a welcome diversion from the more stereotyped roles commonly penned for young women.

Her influence is most seen in the way she influenced a generation of young actresses. Stiles proved that it is possible to effectively shift from adolescent roles to more adult ones, which is a task that many young performers struggle with. Her career choices have shown that young actors may explore a variety of roles while still maintaining a successful career.

An Examination of Her Film and Television Contributions

Stiles' achievements in cinema and television are distinguished by her acting variety and depth. She has shown a remarkable ability to adapt to a wide range of genres in cinema, from romantic comedies to psychological thrillers and action films. Her performances have often been lauded for their sincerity and emotional depth, and she brings a distinct presence to each part she performs.

Stiles had a huge impression on television with her appearance in "Riviera," in which she not only appeared as the primary character but also worked as an executive producer. This work marked her successful entry into television, a medium that has grown in importance in the business. Her work on "Riviera" and other television productions has shown her ability to manage complicated, long-form storytelling, adding another depth to her already illustrious career.

Stiles' Cultural Icon Status

Julia Stiles has become a cultural figure in her own right, further to her work in cinema and television. Her depiction of strong, independent women has struck a chord with both fans and critics, making her a key player in the debate about women's roles in the entertainment business.

Stiles has also been an outspoken supporter of gender equality in Hollywood, speaking out against sexism and advocating for more and better roles for women. Her involvement has made her a role model for both her professional colleagues and her admirers.

Julia Stiles' cinematic career is defined by her great accomplishments as an actor and cultural icon. Her influence on young actors, varied variety of film and television roles, and support for gender equality have made her a powerful presence in Hollywood. Stiles' career demonstrates her skill, flexibility, and dedication to make a difference both on and off the screen.

CONCLUSION

Julia Stiles' career in show business is a fascinating story of adaptability, endurance, and transformation. Her path from a talented child actor to being a teen idol to becoming a renowned actress in both cinema and television is a tribute to her persistent skill and perseverance.

Summary of Professional and Personal Life

Stiles started her acting career in her early twenties, swiftly garnering notoriety in the late 1990s with outstanding parts in films such as "10 Things I Hate About You" and "Wicked," which not only displayed her acting talent but also struck a chord with a generation of young fans. Her entry into adult parts was characterized by her participation in highly praised movies like the "Bourne" series and "Silver Linings Playbook," in which she proved her variety and depth as an actor.

Stiles has had a great personal life in addition to her professional accomplishments. Even at the height of her acting career, her choice to seek further education at Columbia University demonstrates her dedication to personal development and intellectual interests. In her personal life, she has struck a balance between her public and private personas, valuing her roles as a mother and a wife.

The Entertainment Industry's Legacies

Stiles' legacy in the entertainment business is diverse. She is known not just for her vast variety of roles and remarkable performances, but also as a role model for budding performers. She defied stereotypes by demonstrating that transferring from juvenile roles to more sophisticated adult characters is not only doable but also very successful. Her professional decisions have blazed the way for other actors, demonstrating how to traverse the sometimes difficult route of being relevant and real in Hollywood.

Her recent engagement in projects such as "Riviera" and "Hustlers" demonstrates her flexibility to the changing face of the entertainment business. This versatility, along with her steady performances, has earned her a position in Hollywood as a renowned figure.

Stiles' platform has also been used to fight for significant social causes, including gender equality in the film business. Her advocacy effort broadens her reach beyond the screen, making her a role model for both her colleagues and fans.

Reminiscences on Her Living Legacy

When one considers Julia Stiles' career, one cannot but appreciate her not just for her professional accomplishments, but also for how she has behaved herself throughout her career. She has navigated the industry's obstacles while keeping her integrity and remaining faithful to her creative vision.

Her legacy is defined not only by the parts she has done or the awards she has garnered but also by the influence she has had on the business and aspiring performers. Stiles has shown that it is possible to have a successful Hollywood career without sacrificing one's ideals or creative integrity.

Stiles' career offers a remarkable example of endurance and adaptation as the entertainment business evolves. Her rise from adolescent idol to renowned actress in film and television is a model for long-term success in the entertainment business. Her lasting impact reflects her brilliance, tenacity, and dedication to her work.

Finally, Julia Stiles remains an important presence in Hollywood, not just for her various and influential performances, but also for her work off-screen. Her professional trajectory, which has been distinguished by constant development and adaptation, and her personal life, which has been marked by a dedication to education and family, build a picture of an actress who has left an everlasting stamp on the entertainment business.

Printed in Great Britain
by Amazon